SCRIPTURE IN THE STREETS

Reflections on Holy Week, Contemporary Spirituality

Anthony T. Padovano

PAULIST PRESS New York/Mahwah, N.J.

Library of Congress Cataloging-in-Publication Data

Padovano, Anthony T.
    Scripture in the streets : reflections on Holy Week, contemporary spirituality / Anthony T. Padovano.
        p.   cm.
    ISBN 0-8091-3335-0 (pbk.)
        1. Holy Week.   2. Holy Week—Meditations.   3. Retreats.
    4. Spiritual life—Catholic Church.   5. Catholic Church—Membership.
    I. Title.
    BT414.P33   1992
    242'.35—dc20   92-20687
                                                                         CIP

Published by Paulist Press
997 Macarthur Blvd.
Mahwah, N.J. 07430

Printed and bound in the United States of America

CONTENTS

INTRODUCTION

Prophets are found more frequently in the streets than in the temple or the cathedral. In the streets, they encourage or accuse, gather their supporters or lose them. If they become martyrs, they are put to death most frequently in the streets rather than in the churches. And if they prevail, it is because their message is received in the streets.

The young man, Jesus, preached in the fields and in the streets far more often than he did in the temple or synagogue. The only time he wrote was in the streets, in the sands. The intent of this scripture was to stop the violence of an impending execution, to forgive a woman caught in adultery, to indict all accusers with a reminder of how much they were like the sinners they sought to condemn. If we ever needed proof of the power of words, we find it here in this scene. Jesus has no weapons and uses no force to stop the angry mob of, perhaps, well-intentioned, but, more likely, self-righteous, curious and sadistic men. Jesus brings peace and gives life, stops death and banishes violence by using words. In this, he shows himself to be a prophet indeed. The gospel is about the words of Jesus, and Jesus begins the text in the streets, in the sands, with his words and his courage, with his compassion and sensitivity.

Holy Week is the best and the worst of times. The juxtaposition of agony and ecstasy, of guilt and inno-

cence, of horror and hope is so close and so change-
able that one reality continually seems to engender its
opposite. At the end of the turbulence and the terror,
the final meaning is clear. All that is best in the human heart, all that is most worthy of God survives.
The sands of Calvary, the ashes of defeat, have written
in them words of hope and of life. The streets of Jerusalem echo with the declaration that the execution has
been carried out, the crucified is dead; and, then,
soon after, the echoes become the sounds of life: He
is risen; we have seen him, wounded and yet without
pain, scarred with the cross and yet free of it.

This book is a collection of essays and meditations. They were originally conferences and homilies
for a Holy Week retreat organized by the Sisters of
Charity of Convent Station, New Jersey. The unifying
theme is contemporary spirituality and nonviolence in
the light of the passion. Some of the symbols and rituals unique to the retreat are described in an epilogue.
I would like to invite the reader into the drama and
depth of, perhaps, the most moving event in human
history. These pages will make an effort to find a place
for ourselves in the story and to apply it to our time.

To be a Christian is a profound and emotional experience. Seldom is this more undeniable than during
Holy Week. Scripture was a message in the streets before it became a book. We may still have to find it
there if we wish to feel its power and experience its
vitality.

ESSAYS

1

Scripture in the Streets

The woman has no name. She is known only by her crime and her sin. The offense is adultery. The charge is serious. In her day, adultery was more a crime than a sin, though clearly it was both. The penalty is capital punishment. In our day, adultery is more a sin than a crime. The penalty is one's own shame, and often the destruction of a marriage. In her day, adultery brought both shame and death.

The first twelve verses in chapter eight of John's gospel tell the story. A woman is arrested for committing adultery. It is a woman but it does not matter which one. Women had no legal standing, no social position in Israel anyway. And, in this case, the important issue is not the person but the offense. She will be used to make a point, to trap Jesus, to undermine his credibility. Her name, her own feelings matter little. This is not a woman's business. Adultery laws are a question of power and control. They are a man's concern. The debate will bypass the woman, whose life hangs in the balance, as scribes and Pharisees argue a point of law and authority with Jesus. Her death is an irrelevance. This is, as the passage tells us, "a test," a question of evidence "for something to use against him." The debate opens with the language of power. Moses is invoked, the ultimate legal reference. "You see, Master, Moses ordered us in the law to condemn. . . ." Author-

5

ity, law, condemnation, orders. Somehow they fit conveniently together. The woman, she is a person of little consequence. Her death is merely the way the system works, the price a few pay for the order and, perhaps, the comfort the system requires.

Most scripture scholars agree that this passage does not belong here. Indeed, it is not in the style of John's gospel. It probably is better placed in Luke's gospel, very likely at the end of chapter 21 or at the beginning of chapter 22. Its position there is important, as we shall see, because it begins the passion narrative. Since practically everyone agrees with this judgment about the text, why don't we? Clearly, this material is very much like Luke who stresses forgiveness and accents the role of women in the gospel. And its writing style is consistent with Luke's gospel as we know it.

If this be the case, it completes the circle, so to speak. Matthew, Mark and John, all begin their account of the passion of Christ with the story of a woman. Only Luke does not begin the passion narrative with a woman's story and yet he was always sensitive to the place of women.

Matthew, Mark and John tell their story differently, but it is always a woman who begins the passion narrative with an anointing. The place is Bethany in all three gospels. The oil is poured on the head of Jesus in Matthew and Mark, and Jesus declares that what this anonymous woman has done will be told in memory of her. In John, it is Martha's sister Mary who anoints and she anoints not the head but the feet of Jesus. Matthew, Mark and John all observe that this was done for the burial of Jesus. And so the passion narrative, the heart of the gospel, begins with a woman in three of the four gospels.

Luke, however, does not begin with a woman. He tells a similar story early in his gospel (chapter 7) about "a woman . . . who had a bad name in the town." She weeps and anoints the feet of Jesus with oil and tears and kisses and her hair. The point of Luke's story, however, is not about the burial of Jesus but about forgiveness. It has no immediate reference to the passion narrative. Jesus forgives the anonymous woman and invites her to "go in peace." Luke's story is less about Jesus than it is about the forgiveness of the woman, less about his burial than it is about her life. The incident is socially embarrassing for Jesus because he is in the home of a Pharisee and the woman is a public sinner. Nonetheless, Jesus thinks not of himself but of her.

In any case, when Luke composes his passion narrative, there is no woman to begin it. He, most of all, would have begun in this manner. But he does not.

Or so we once thought. If the passage in John 8:1–12 belongs not to John's gospel but to Luke's, then we have completed the circle. All the evangelists introduce the passion narratives with the story of a woman. And so did Luke, before the passage got shifted to John's eighth chapter. If this be true, Luke's beginning of the passion with a woman's story is the most dramatic.

Let us now go beyond the scriptural exegesis and follow the story line.

It is early morning and Jesus is in the temple, the greatest symbol of power and authority in Israel. He feels a little out of place. He prefers the gentle seashore or the restless waters of the Sea of Galilee. He seems more at home on roads or in quiet mountains. The temple and the city are not the place where the preaching and parables of Jesus seem to work best.

The temple is a hard place for a prophet to be. This is the temple of the priests with all the solidity of law and tradition behind it. Nonetheless, he begins to teach, with his impending death in the air. And people gather to hear the young prophet.

Some of the Pharisees arrive, those most hostile to him. Jesus by now knew their faces and sensed the danger. They have in tow a woman just arrested for adultery.

It must have been a dreadful moment for her. It is early morning. The woman is dragged from where she slept, scarcely dressed, mortified, caught in sin, beginning to tremble because the end of her life is only moments away. Angry men push and shove her through the streets.

This is a violent story, filled with shock and shame. And it raises, as all violent stories do, disturbing questions about the victim and about us. One must always choose sides in a violent story. There are no neutral places to stand.

The Pharisees are cruel. They treat the woman as an object. They exploit and rape her psychologically. They make her "stand there in full view of everybody." Visualize the scene. Put yourself in her place, in their place, in the place of Jesus, in our place. It is not a story anymore. It is an event. A choice has to be made. Courage and cowardice, compassion and compromise become seductive and incessant possibilities. There is no way out except by choice. A life hangs in the balance, in the choosing. The atmosphere is charged with violence. It is not a moment for timid spirits.

"Master, this woman was caught in the very act of committing adultery and Moses has ordered us in the law to condemn women like this." She is pointed out in a gesture of contempt. She is most likely shivering in fear and shame, her body reflecting the panic and despair of her heart. The last sounds she will hear are the sounds of taunting, rejection, riducule.

As Jesus hears of Moses and the law, his memory recalls Leviticus 20:10 which orders death for the man who commits adultery with a married woman. She must also die. Leviticus is clear that, for a man, adultery can only happen with a married woman.

At the time of Jesus, adultery is interpreted as a property question rather than a sexual one. A married man did not commit adultery, as he does in our society, if he sleeps with a single woman. But a married woman did commit adultery if she slept with a single man. Why? Because a married woman is always someone's property, and that property is violated whether a married or a single man commits adultery with her. But a single woman is no one's marital property and, therefore, if a man, married or single sleeps with her, no adultery is incurred. A man can only commit adultery if his partner is already married or betrothed to be married.

The manner of execution is not prescribed in Leviticus but stoning was always assumed if no manner of death is specified.

Deuteronomy 22:22–23 is less vague. "If a man is caught sleeping with another man's wife, both must die. . . . If a virgin is betrothed and a man meets her in the city and sleeps with her," they must be stoned to death.

The woman had heard these words as a young girl. She may have remembered them at times during the affair. They seal her doom now.

Executions are usually rituals of convenience. Since Israel has a rocky and stony terrain, stoning became the most common form of execution. It was different elsewhere. The Law of Hammurabi called most frequently for drowning the condemned rather than stoning because Babylonia, present-day Iraq, had the Tigris and Euphrates rivers nearby. Executions, as we have said, are rituals of convenience.

Stoning was often done outside the town where more stones were accessible. The witnesses of the crime threw the first stones and began the killing. It was all carefully scripted. These were favored places for execution, killing fields, where people would gather. The stoning was a community action. It was a male prerogative. No one knew who struck the fatal blow and so the entire company of men took responsibility for it. The bones were crushed, the head destroyed. It was not a pleasant task to remove the body after the execution.

According to the law, stoning did not technically entail the shedding of blood so that blood guilt or ritual pollution did not follow. One could kill purely if stoning was the manner of inflicting death. It was a good way for the scrupulous to kill.

The language of the Pharisees is sharp and strikes Jesus like a rough stone. Moses is the ultimate lawgiver, the final authority and arbiter. He has ordered us, the Pharisees say, to condemn women like this. The language is belligerent. It gives the woman no hope and Jesus no chance to save her with compassion. It is a hard moment, setting the stage, it seems, for a hard death.

"What have you to say?" they insist. Jesus cannot be an onlooker. He must decide for them, for her. Jesus will seal his fate if he sets her free. Who would dare set himself above Moses? It is an appropriate story to begin the passion.

Jesus begins to write on the ground, in the sand. He writes where the woman's body is to be crushed. He does not speak. There is an ominous silence, the first silence the woman has heard since her arrest.

The passage says that "they persisted with their questions." "What have you to say?" "Why do you not answer?"

And then the words that cut through the violence and silence all accusers. "If there is one of you who has not sinned, let him be the first to throw a stone at her." He continues to write on the ground.

It is dreadful to stand between a crowd ready to kill and the victim. It is worse when the crowd is convinced God will be glorified by such a grisly death. What would lead Jesus to endanger himself? For a woman? For an adulteress? Why risk so much for one so unworthy? Some might justify the killing by arguing that religion needs defense, from time to time, with violence.

"If there is one of you who has not sinned, let him be the first to throw a stone at her." The executioners begin to leave, "one by one," the passage notes, "beginning with the eldest." Soon only Jesus is left, and the woman. He does not leave because he is not an accuser.

What were her thoughts as she watched them leave, still uncertain if a few might stay? It only takes a few to kill a woman. What were her thoughts about Jesus?

Pacifism requires courage and a willingness to die, certainly to suffer, clearly to have one's standing in the community imperiled.

Finally, after a long time, Jesus looks directly at her. She sees the face of her deliverer. Even if she had seen him on a previous occasion she sees him differently now. The one who delivers us has a face we did not see before in the same way.

"Woman, where are they?" "Has no one condemned you?"

"No one, sir." These are the only words she speaks in the passage.

"Neither do I condemn you . . . go and sin no more."

The passion story begins with an act of compassion. It begins on a note of pacifism. The violence will come later. For now, freedom and forgiveness win out. This anonymous woman is all of us who may have compromised our ideals. Jesus asks that we not be violent with one another or with ourselves. Jesus treats her with respect. He has rescued her because she is worthy of love.

On trembling legs, the woman walks away from death. It is Easter for her before Good Friday has even happened.

2

Bread and Roses

It is Thursday.

The scene is not the temple or the streets; the players are not the Pharisees or an anonymous woman. A dinner is being prepared. It is an intimate setting.

Intimacy functions in different modalities. There is an intimacy even in violence, since violence is a forceful entry into another life at the deepest level of its vitality. There is intimacy also in nonviolence, since the conscience is confronted and our vulnerability to change and conversion is addressed. The dinner we consider, however, is intimate because of the friendship and trust of those who gather to share it.

The passion narrative began with a woman who, rescued and forgiven, walked away anonymously into the streets of Jerusalem. The event is a parable of death and resurrection, a death averted as she is raised up from the earth and restored. It is only Luke who gives us this account, granted the scriptural problem we have discussed already. It is only Luke who gives us the story of another anonymous sinner, the good thief on the cross. He, too, is saved at the last moment and given a promise of spiritual life and paradise. The companions of Jesus on the journey are often the unnamed sinners who are ready for grace if someone will show them mercy.

The disciples prepare the passover dinner with memories of the adulterous woman and the hostile Pharisees. As they purchase bread and wine, the lamb and herbs, as they seek out a house for the supper, they can hear those words, somehow intrusive and healing at the same time, like a surgeon's knife: "If there is one of you who has not sinned, let him begin the killing." The only one capable of declaring himself sinless, the only one licensed by his own standard to throw the first stone, is prevented by his very sinlessness from killing. We shall see on Friday how the innocence of Jesus makes him both impotent and omnipotent.

The disciples come to the supper as future participants will be expected to join it, with sins as well as hopes, with memories of violence from the past and forgiveness in the present. There is room at the dinner for the adulterous woman rescued from death and for the dying thief promised paradise.

The words and deeds of Jesus lodge in the conscience like a stone, an intrusion which wounds and heals. It is not pain or suffering which defines violence; violence is pain and suffering given or received without love. Nonviolence is not painless; the passover supper is not without suffering.

Every life-giver inflicts pain; there is no way to allow birth without suffering to the fetus, no way to nurture the young without some measure of constraint and discipline, no way to sustain marriages or friendships without inflicting our inadequacies on others. It is not pain which defines violence but pain which intends no healing, pain which excludes love and rejects the other. Pacifism is not the absence of pain; it is simply the companion of love.

The disciples may have been deeply disturbed by their memories of the impending execution of the adulterous woman. They may have approved of it and desired it until Jesus stopped the killing. As children they may have witnessed such happenings and been assured that God sanctioned such behavior.

The Pharisees may have been troubled by their memories of the same incident. They may have asked themselves through a night of restlessness what their real motives were in apprehending the woman and why a few words from Jesus kept them from doing what the law required. .

The memories may have been painful for the woman who must now leave her former lover and the previous definitions she had of who she was.

The memories may have been unsettling for Jesus, who realizes that his death will not long be delayed after this bold challenge to the law and the temple, after this prophetic confrontation with the religious system of his day and the social structures of domination and power.

Nonviolence is not cost-free; it is not cheap grace; it takes away our comfort and causes pain.

It is not an easy passover for the disciples to prepare. There is so much to bring to it.

What do we bring to such a supper? We deserve no place at this table unless we come with disturbing memories and dangerous hopes, willing to exchange yesterday's false securities for today's forgiveness.

Pacifism is not essentially a tactic or a technique. A technique works even if the person supposedly benefiting from the technique is given little attention. A technique is sometimes a monologue by the technician rather than a dialogue with the other. A technique is often believed in even if there is little faith in people.

Pacifism is not born of tactics and techniques. It is

generated by insight into the human heart and by intimate connections of friendship and community.

Jesus spoke to the adulterous woman and to her accusers. He did not devise a tactic or a technique. These would not have been inappropriate but they are not prior in importance. Jesus had an insight into a woman's heart and into the spirits of the accusers; he addressed her humanity and theirs; he offered all of them the option of nonviolence, a life free of the need to kill, a soul cleansed of the poison of anger and hatred, a future without adultery or betrayal, self-righteousness or legal cruelty.

Nonviolence allows us to see the other and to identify with the other. It makes the whole world a passover supper table. It has bread for everyone. Jesus did not send away the men ready to execute the woman; he merely asked that they abandon their weapons; they left on their own accord. But there are places for them at the table, as long as they are willing to turn their stones in for bread.

Pacifism cannot live without community. No community can survive unless it is nonviolent. Violence, however, does not need a community. In a sense, each killer is an isolated person. Every act of violence is an experience of segregation and seclusion.

When people enter marriage, they vow not to be defined without the intimate community of the other and they choose the possibility of children and family. The vow of marriage is, in effect, a vow of nonviolence.

Adultery is an assault on this nonviolence and on the community between two people. It brings to the marital table, not the bread of harmony but the stones of discord, not the new wine of nonviolence but the old wineskins of belligerence.

In a similar manner, the vows made in formal religious communities, vows of poverty, virginity and obedience, are vows of nonviolence. The vows do not intend frugality, celibacy and submission primarily, but they do intend community. Every community is essentially nonviolent or else it ceases to exist. Violence makes a community a commune of detached individuals who pursue, at best, a project or even, ironically, an ideal.

If the passion story is a narrative of nonviolence and community, it is fitting that it begin with the nonviolence of forgiving the adulterous woman and with the community celebration of a passover meal.

It is at the passover supper that Jesus will speak of vine and branches, of a unity so vital that violence becomes impossible. No vine is at war with its branches.

Jesus ends the passover in John's gospel with the astonishing words that the intent of his life is that "I may be in them." In this harmony, all notions of violence between God and the human family are dispelled; the violence which alienates ourselves from our own humanity is to be dropped like a stone.

The gospel assures us that deep in our humanity God abides and Christ is present as the sinless core of our existence, as that which makes us endlessly capable of forgiveness and love. All violence emerges from a hatred of ourselves; it seeks the destruction of the other as a way of annihilating the self.

As Jesus breaks bread, he gives us roses as well.

Bread is for the body. We must not live on bread alone, we are told. Bread is eaten best in community, around the family table of our loyalties and friends. In community, bread reaches the heart and the spirit and frees us from the isolation which leads to adulteries and betrayals. The community forgives us our sins, in part by making it less likely that we shall sin. It ends our hostilities by giving us its friendship. The community which gives us bread tells us that it wants us to go on living and to remain present with it. Bread is for the body. It does its work as we consume it in community and enter into communion with bread itself and with all those around the table.

Roses are for the spirit. The rose is not for consumption but for contemplation. It fills us with awe and keeps us at a physical distance. It is a transcendent symbol.

We offer one another bread out of necessity as well as choice. We give roses as an act of luxury and extravagance, as a tribute to the heart and the dignity of the other. Roses are as prodigal and lavish as forgiveness for an adulterous woman, or as a promise to love someone for better or for worse forever, or as a vow of virginity, or as God dying for us. A rose stays in the memory indelibly, long after it has perished; it renews the spirit with invincible vitality.

The passover supper is a rose for the community of faith. It is a mysterious, elusive, somehow distant as well as intimate souvenir of love. It is sacrament as memory, and experience as hope. It nourishes us long after the bread is gone and the wine exhausted. It is the Christian community's most joyful celebration of forgiveness, of bonding or marriage or covenant with God. It is the gospel in bread and wine. It is a faint but real sign of what it would be like if we loved one another without ceasing and if we ended all violence forever.

When Dante contemplated heaven in his *Divine Comedy,* he envisioned it as a rose of light. God was the essence of the rose just as Christ is the essence of the bread. The wine of the Spirit brings us bread and roses. The bread of Christ gives us the nearness of the divine, a nearness so intimate that it delivers us and forgives us and enters into community with us. Christ becomes the vine of all our branches. The spirit also brings us the rose of God who is less accessible and yet somehow marvelously close.

Passover is a feast of bread and roses. It finds a place for everyone at the table—for Judas who betrays and for Peter who denies. The enemy is invited so that the enemy might become the friend through the transubstantiation of forgiveness and community. The supper is the place where our feet are washed and bread is broken for us; we are given wine and roses which die for us even as we hold them. Passover is sacrifice and celebration as both of them conspire to give us life.

The New Testament gives us no assurance that there were women at the last supper. Women begin the passion narratives with anointing and with the acceptance of forgiveness. They stand by the cross and they come first to the empty tomb. Their place at the passover table is less explicit. They may, of course, have baked the bread and set the table. What matters is not whether they were there, but whether a eucharistic celebration which excludes women is proper.

In any case, we might invite to the table some women in the present century who have made the gospel and nonviolence believable.

DOROTHY DAY

One of the women might be Dorothy Day, a woman who could be charged with adultery and abortion but who believed Christ had forgiven her on both

19

counts. She is the woman in the circle of angry accusers whom Christ pardons of all offenses.

Dorothy was a woman of the streets in a manner different from the negative implications of that term. She wanted to return Christ to the streets, to liberate him from the temple and churches where Christians imprison him. "Christ no longer walks the streets of this world . . .," Dorothy once observed sadly.

Christ walks the streets of this world, for Dorothy, if he is a prophet of nonviolence. She would not choose sides in the Spanish Civil War or in World War II, even though these wars were seen by most Catholics as holy wars. There were no holy wars, she argued, and no expendable lives. Every death on either side was for her a stoning in the streets.

Dorothy deserves a place at the table of the Lord, next to the Twelve.

She lived in the slums and walked the streets of poverty and despair bringing bread and roses for people who were starving and who had not been given a flower or a gift for as long as they could remember.

Dorothy Day was imprisoned for the first time in 1917 as she marched in protest for women's right to vote. That experience changed her life. She identified with those in prison, much as Jesus identified with the woman imprisoned by hatred and impending death because of her adultery. She gives a graphic description of her first prison experience in her autobiography, *From Union Square to Rome:*

> I was no longer a young girl . . . I was the oppressed. I was that drug addict, screaming and tossing in her cell . . . I was that mother whose child had been raped and slain. I was the mother who had borne the monster who had done it. I

was even that monster, feeling in my heart every abomination.

These words resound with the New Testament proclamation of the Christ who bore all our sins.

Surely, there is a place for Dorothy at the last supper. Who would deny her room at the table? Should there not be a place for such women at the table and the inns of the world? Who would presume to offer her a lesser place, merely because she is a woman or a lay person?

This woman who brought bread to the hungry and roses to the depressed deserves a place at the table and in the paradise prepared for those who identified with the least of Christ's sisters and brothers.

Robert Coles, the Harvard University professor and Pulitzer Prize author, writes of his first meeting with Dorothy Day.

Dorothy Day was talking to an alcoholic woman. There was an interminable, absurd exchange of ranting and silent nodding. As Robert Coles waited to interview Dorothy, he became impatient. Brief questions from Dorothy would wind up this over-talkative woman time and again. Finally silence ensued. Dorothy noticed that Robert Coles was watching. She asked the woman if she would mind an interruption. She approached Coles and asked him a question which startled him. "Are you waiting to talk to one of us?" To "one of us!" How absurd and how Christ-like! The anonymous and wounded woman had been given bread at Dorothy's table. She was also gifted with the roses of Dorothy's respect and companionship.

How could a woman who identified so thoroughly with others ever be violent? Dorothy saw everyone as "one of us." Jesus saw the woman taken in adultery as "one of us." He gave her the time and attention, as Dorothy did her companion, when others chose to demean and dismiss her.

Let us invite other women to the table.

Dorothy went to prison in 1917. Five years earlier, in 1912, a group of women in Lawrence, Massachusetts, inaugurated a new chapter in the annals of human rights.

The textile mills of Lawrence were, in effect, prisons where people were degraded and exploited. As women labored to support their families, they were denied bread and roses. The factories, where they worked 56 hours a week destroyed bodies as well as spirits. The pay for those long hours was $8.76 a week.

One day, 20,000 women spontaneously left the mills, each following the other as word spread. They went into the streets, refusing to work. The women feared that they would be dealt with violently, and sent their children away for safety but also to spare their children the sight of their mothers being killed.

The strike was managed by a democratically-elected "Committee of 56 Women," representing, of course, the 56-hour week. Women were not allowed to vote in the United States in 1912, but they could vote for one another and did during the strike. The committee found interpreters for the 27 languages spoken by the mostly poor, immigrant women so that not a single person was uninformed about the strike or the issues they were asked to decide by vote.

The International Workers of the World declared the strike not only an effective action for labor reform but an event which led people to believe in humanity at its best. The first strike by women has been judged the most impressive strike in American history and the one most democratically managed.

A few young women carried "Bread and Roses" placards. Joseph Oppenheim wrote a poem around those words and Caroline Kohlsaat set it to music.

"Bread and Roses" was sung for ten weeks until the nonviolent strike ended and 250,000 textile workers returned to the mills of New England.

The lyrics of this anthem spoke of pacifism and community. The women sang that men, since they are women's children, too, must also share in the bread and roses which belonged to all people. The words tell of art and love and beauty and ask that the rising of women might help the whole human family rise.

"Bread and Roses" is an Easter hymn rising from the calvary of the textile mills. It is sung bravely in the shadows of the factories and crosses of Lawrence, Massachusetts.

Surely, these women deserve a place at the table. They are the sisters and daughters of the woman taken in adultery, rejected and despised as she was, marginalized by society and yet the center of Christ's concern.

Who would dare send them from the table or assign them a lesser place?

How joyous an occasion it was as the women, singing "Bread and Roses," welcomed back the children they had not seen for weeks!

The last supper is not a meal only. It is a community, a home and a table for all aliens and sinners. We must not take bread here unless we discard our stones. We do not deserve to sit with Christ unless we preach him in the streets and find him in the marginalized women, the desperate soup kitchens and depressing mills of the world. To all these we are expected to bring bread and roses, justice and peace.

Jesus Christ is the bread of the passover meal but also the rose of Calvary; he is the wheat of the last supper but also the flower of Easter morning. In Christ, there is now neither Jew nor Gentile, slave nor free, male nor female, fear, violence nor oppression.

The table has a place for everyone; the bread is broken for all; and roses are denied no one.

3

Death in the Afternoon

To stand with those society rejects is a perilous business. It is even more hazardous, when rejection is reinforced with religious language.

There is an inescapable connection between the woman condemned for adultery (a crime in the civil order; a sin in the religious sphere) and the crucifixion of the Jesus who rescues her. Mercy is easier for a culture to countenance when it remains within recognizable legal and ethical boundaries. Jesus surpasses those limits in aiding the woman.

Pacifism becomes problematic for many because it ventures beyond conventional categories. Wars, for example, are often legal and may even be called ethical or just wars. Since people generally fear chaos more than violence, they accept war, for the most part, as an inevitability or even an imperative. On the cross, we see someone who does not remain within these tolerable bounds.

The cross has become so conventional, our love for the crucified so intense that we diminish the challenge the crucifixion poses for us. The proximity of Easter in our consciousness lessens the horror and the confrontation.

Had we been at the trial, would we have voted to release Jesus? Think of it. To sit in the Sanhedrin was to have a place of high honor. One had a stake, an investment, so to speak, in the structures of that culture. Institutions, understandably, give rewards to those who support the system. None of this is necessarily evil or even compromising, at least in the beginning. Society does need structures and good people exist at the highest levels of all institutions. Promotion, election, office, honor, prestige are not bad in themselves. They are, of course, dangerous. They tend to imprison us, define us, confine us, neutralize us.

The rationalizations we sometimes contrive to work within the system are not unreasonable. I can do more good, we argue, if I work within an institution and if I am acceptable to large numbers of people than if I become a prophet, a marginalized person, a voice crying in the wilderness, a critic.

And so the process begins.

The Sanhedrin was the Senate and Supreme Court of its day. People noticed Sanhedrin members in the market place. One became a hero to one's children. The public listened when a member of the Sanhedrin spoke. Everyone knew who you were and seemed to care about you.

The Sanhedrin did a lot of good. With a Roman army on Israeli soil, with Gentiles crowding the streets of Jerusalem, with a representative of Caesar rather than a Jewish king in Judea, the Sanhedrin became the major influence in keeping the Torah and the law, the prophets and the temple free from contamination.

If we sat in the Sanhedrin, we would have a clear sense of our own importance, of our career achievements, of our need to uphold the tradition, of how many people depended on us to be exactly who we were and to do what we were doing.

Is it not like this now, for many of us?

All well and good, as we say.

Jesus is suddenly brought before this assembly. Why, just a day or two ago, he let a woman caught in adultery go free. Is this not a way of condoning sexual license? Are our young people not already corrupted by Gentile standards, by the music and the morals and the money of the modern world?

If such women go free, what signal does this give to decent people? What would happen to honorable marriage, to a relationship we see as a sign of our covenant with God? If women can make choices as she did, if they have such options, how could men be certain that women will behave as they should? Moreover, men are weak. What might we do, even we, ourselves, members of the Sanhedrin, if other men's wives were available and we thought we could get away with it?

Is it not like this now, for many of us?

Let us think about it.

If we permit homosexuals to use church facilities, if we insist on their civil rights, if we demand that they be treated fairly, would this not seem as though we were condoning sin? Would this permissiveness be equivalent to saying there are no moral limits? Jesus seemed to be doing the same thing when he told the woman accused of adultery that there need not be punishments or harsh consequences of her sin. Can people learn morality if they are not punished? Is "go in peace and sin no more" enough when we are dealing with serious and publicly known sinfulness?

If people can make sexual choices in our day about the gender of their partners, or in Jesus' day about whether the partner is married or not, what sexual norms would remain? Did not God condemn sodomy in Sodom as surely as God condemned adultery in the Torah?

Even though one may encounter an occasional homosexual who seems to be decent, is it not fitting that each and every one be punished so that the entire people not perish? Some apparently honorable women may commit adultery, but if we allow such people to go unvilified, what will people think of the lax standards of their religious leaders? Will they think we are adulterers too? If we defend homosexuals, will people suspect our own orientation?

Nasty business, this.

It is not easy sitting in the Sanhedrin. There is a lot to defend; and one must be careful not to offend.

How would we have voted?

Jesus told us we were to treat others as we would want to be treated. We reduce the commandment to rhetoric so easily. We rationalize that Jesus would have acted harshly if he had to face what we do now; we assume that our society, our church, our problems are more complex and perilous than those faced by Jesus. People must not become impatient, we argue, with our inability to take the commandment of love seriously. Someday we shall get there. Not now. Justice delayed is not justice denied.

If we let things take their course, if we get too tenderhearted, the whole system will go. Since people are heavily invested in immorality, since they are essentially lawbreakers, since they are, for the most part, laity, with no training or position in the church, with no sense of responsibility for the tradition or the various factions and constituencies which must be balanced, since they are such people, why should we take them seriously?

Just a few days ago, we presented to Jesus just such a person, a woman taken in adultery. He took her part. What does he know anyway? He is a layman. He is not a priest. Which rabbi taught him? He comes from Galilee. What do Galileans know?

The woman in adultery? We would have killed her, of course. We are not animals or demons and so we would have felt something for her. We have wives and daughters. It is awful to hear such women when the large stones smash against their heads. We are not insensitive; we are merely responsible. We are officers and leaders of the Jewish people. It is not always an enviable position although no one of us ever seems to resign. The people need us too much.

The woman should have been killed. In the long run, it would have been better for everyone. A little violence now prevents anarchy later.

How would we have voted had we been on the Sanhedrin?

Jesus keeps making life uncomfortable for us. It is only human to distance ourselves from those who make us uncomfortable. Indeed, it may even be divine when those who make us uncomfortable threaten God's position in the universe.

We are primarily interested in God's law. Sometimes people get in the way of this. Or, as we might say it at a later date, we are, above all, committed to Christ's cause. No one should be allowed to be an obstacle or a scandal.

We may not want certain people showing up in Sanhedrins or Chancery offices, in rectories or convents. If you were an officer of the people, would you want your picture taken with a homosexual or an adulterer, a censured theologian or a married priest, an African-American agitator or a lawbreaking pacifist? Be reasonable. How would all this look in the Jerusalem morning newspaper? What might they say in Rome? Caesar, we all know, can remove anyone from office.

And, so, Jesus is before us. How do we feel? A little angry at him for making us feel conflicted. But, thank God, Jesus makes our task easy. He has practically nothing to offer in his defense. The charges against him are serious and irrefutable. He is tongue-tied, reduced to silence. No prophetic histrionics and theatrics. Silence. Understandable, of course. How can anyone defend what he did? We have Moses on our side. There is no legal way to justify such behavior. He knows neither law nor theology and was, therefore, especially inept. A lay type. And, from Galilee.

When he did speak, he spoke outrageously. He did himself no good. He attacked the temple and seemed to exalt himself above Moses. He acts as though he were God.

Such people, in later centuries, might wonder if the pope is wrong and might attack the curia, the Vatican, the councils, church teaching. It is better to stop it in the beginning. Or, one day, women may want to sit in the Sanhedrin or make laws for their own lives or do temple service.

We know what kind of temple service women do in those other religions. Stop it in the beginning.

Women might deal with the law with more emotion or compassion than is healthy. We may not want them making judgments about married priests or homosexuals or whether to give communion to those who do not obey all our laws or even exist outside our organizations. Stop it in the beginning. Nip it in the bud. Otherwise who knows where all this will take us?

If a few women are denied their rights, if a few priests are forbidden their options, if a few theologians are censured, if some newspapers are censored and a few books condemned, if an occasional war is justified and a few criminals put to death, if selected homosexuals are vilified and a few parishes closed because there are not enough male celibates to serve them, if angry Catholics reject our sexual teaching (what would they know about it anyway?) and walk away, if some people are refused communion and made to feel unwelcome in church, if those who never deserved to be one of us leave, if the whole is purified by the departure of the polluted and the self-indulgent, if some of the laity are not heard and none of them allowed to vote, if there are painful decisions we have to make and these decisions inflict enormous pain on a few and destroy a life or a reputation, a ministry or a career here or there, if all this happens, well, it happens to be the way the world is. And the church, you see, is no different. Admittedly, we might react with less objectivity if the few who are to suffer were ourselves but, nonetheless, those who obey the rules need not fear.

Jesus before the Sanhedrin may have seemed not wise enough to know the consequences of what he had been saying and doing. And, so, Judaism may have needed protection from Jesus just as later Christianity would sometimes seek to protect itself from the radical demands of Jesus and the prophetic naiveté of those who keep appealing to Jesus as a norm for the church. Some Christian communities search out legal substitutes for Jesus, infallible guides who know more about the New Testament than those who wrote it, more about the Christian community than those who belong to it.

If we in the Sanhedrin, get rid of Jesus now we shall do the future a favor. We shall keep the lawbreakers and the fanatics, the visionaries and the zealots from having an advocate.

It is not, you see, easy to sit in the Sanhedrin. We

31

must judge not only for the present but for all future ages. That is what infallible leaders do. This is what those who speak unerringly in God's name are expected to accomplish. Nothing less than God's truth for all time, irreversible and unfailing.

We must be careful not to scandalize the little ones, the ignorant, the faithful supporters of the system. We must reinforce those who keep our laws and their vows. The system is important; sometimes more important than the people in it. Surely, no one in Israel or Rome doubts that.

People need and desire clear guidelines, courageous leadership, visible limits, defined doctrines, unambiguous laws, certitude and eternal norms. Without such supports, they wander and lose their way.

Jesus before the Sanhedrin will be followed many centuries later by Gandhi before British justice in India. What do Indians know about India or about what is good for them? Jesus before the Sanhedrin is followed by Native Americans. If American Indians, it was argued, were allowed to prevail, with their lack of hygiene and ethics, with their pagan practices and savagery, how could the nation go forward? Jesus before the Sanhedrin is followed by Martin Luther King, Jr. What do African Americans know about their place in the larger scheme of things? African Americans are tolerant with adultery and those who break the law; they are lazy and arrogant with the white majority. They make life uncomfortable for those who feel responsible for order and justice in society. They make slums of American cities and a mockery of its educational system. This would be a much more impressive nation if Indians and African Americans, if other diverse groups and deviant types were not on the scene.

Jesus before the Sanhedrin. Sitting there we might

reason that Judaism is a marvelous religion if only Jesus would leave it to responsible Jews. What does he know, we might observe, about what Judaism is supposed to be?

At a later date, women will want to define their own role in society and church. They will agitate, self-indulgently, for their own ordination. They will press this demand in spite of all previous tradition and present law. If Jesus wanted women ordained he would have provided for them.

The burdens men bear! The complexities of being on the Sanhedrin and the curia! Why do so many think it is simple? It's never as simple as Jesus made it out to be. The simpleminded ask: what would Jesus do? Would Jesus do this? As if they knew! As if he knew! As if we do not know! Do they think we care less than they about Jesus or the community, about ethics or them? We are not animals or demons, you see. Just men—and, of course, *just* men.

Why did Jesus set the woman taken in adultery free? This assault on the system was worse than his attack on the money changers. Jesus goes too far. Prophets and reformers always do.

Consider Luther. He went too far, didn't he? And Gandhi. He wanted to determine the destiny of an entire subcontinent. American Indians wanted a continent. And Martin Luther King, Jr., wanted justice for those who had earned the right. Sooner or later, the prophets and reformers ask for too much.

Dorothy Day claimed every war was intrinsically evil and that Christians should never bear arms. What did she know? What seminary took her in and approved of her?

Women strikers in Lawrence, Massachusetts! What did they know about economics or managing a textile mill? They were given jobs and, ungratefully, wanted more. Bread and roses! How cute! Just what you'd expect women to say.

The critics of the system are never grateful. We give them jobs and they join unions. When did American Indians thank the United States for the reservations and the government benefits? African Americans are offered subsidized housing and they ruin it. We build clinics and they come in with narcotic addictions.

Jesus went too far. He came out of Galilee with nothing and we let him preach in the synagogues and teach in the temple. We sent our best and our brightest to debate him. We let him go a few years, hoping he'd come to his senses. But he didn't and so he's here—on trial.

We've spent enough time with this Jesus. Let's make a decision. If we're in doubt, the chief priest will decide for us. It's good to have infallible chief priests for, well, the ambiguous moments. We of the Sanhedrin will not rescue the vulnerable or the victims if the chief priest becomes angry and tears his tunic.

Let's vote on Jesus. It isn't easy. You know there were some things we liked about him. He did care about God—a little too much, perhaps. And some of his stories lodged in our memories and consciences like a stone.

Let's make a decision. It's easier if the people we send to death are not like us. It would be harder to order the execution of a member of the Sanhedrin than the death of a woman or an agitator or a Galilean or an American Indian or an African American or a homosexual or a rabble-rousing striking mob of people singing about Bread and Roses.

Let's make a decision.

Crucify him! Destroy him! Kill him for not letting us kill that adulteress.

Eliminate him and save the temple. Execute him and save the law. Convict him and rescue our doctrine. Dismiss him so that our liturgy can be pure. Denounce him in the name of God.

Hang him on a tree—with all the Blacks he would have saved. Kill him in the streets—with all the women he would have rescued. Nail him to a cross—with all the critics he would have defended. Whip him and beat him into submission—call in the police or the military to club him until he has some sense or until he is silent for good—for the good of us all.

Pilate's wife pleads for him. Ignore her. What does she know? If the women of Jerusalem weep for him, pay them no attention. If the laity and the crowds grieve for him, allow them their tears but nothing else. We in the Sanhedrin know whose pain is important and whose pain is less worthy.

Hang him on a tree—for not being grateful, for not knowing his place, for not knowing ours.

And so it is done. We have voted. He is doomed.

Jesus didn't make it easy for us. He prayed for his executioners, and asked for their forgiveness even as they nailed him to the cross. Damn it, Jesus. Have a heart. Die easy.

Forgive *us!* Who was he to forgive us? Did he think he was God or even right? He never admitted he was wrong. Imagine! Those of you who are without sin may throw the first stones.

We may honor him a bit if he is dead. But he must be dead first.

Was defending a woman apprehended in adultery worth your death, Jesus? You had no sense—no proportion. You were so politically naive. You didn't know the limits or the rules.

Had Jesus lived what would have been left of Judaism?

Those of you who condemn the Sanhedrin decision would have voted as we did had you been in our place. Can't you see that?

It's over now. Forget it. It's finished.

We will say this about him: he died without anger. He did not curse us from the cross. Perhaps he understood why we had to do what we did.

When Jesus died, we put him in the arms of his mother. We are not animals, you see. We did not want him dead—only silent—out of the way. But he would not go.

When Jesus died, one member of the Sanhedrin arranged for the burial and gave him a tomb. We are not animals, you see.

We allowed his mother to stand beneath the cross. She washed his feet with her tears. The grief on her face as she held him for the last time—a little as she held him in his birth—the grief was devastating. We did not want her hurt. She was not a problem for us. But there was no way to kill him without unintended consequences, collateral damage so to speak.

It is all exquisitely sad. He could have saved himself if he had gone away or taught in a more conventional manner or submitted a little.

You see, he really killed himself. If you act in a certain way, you become your own worst enemy. All of a sudden, there isn't room for you any more in the inn or the Sanhedrin, in the temple or the church. The only room left is on the cross, outside the city, far from the sanctuary, a long way from the clerical positions of power.

When we took him down from the cross, we didn't know where to put him. So we put him in his mother's arms. We're not animals, you see.

Wouldn't you have done what we did? Have you not done so already? Think about it, not sentimentally but carefully.

The two worst moments were getting him out of his mother's arms and getting her away from the tomb. She's probably still there, waiting. When a mother buries her child, the vigil never ends.

It is better. You will see. We gave him a decent burial. It is time now to attend to other matters.

You would have done what we did. Think about it!

4

Vigil

We must not have hearts of stone. The stones for executing the woman must fall from our hands. In place of stones, God will give us bread.

The hammers made to crucify Jesus are made of stone. He must not become for us a stone in our hands to use against one another. For, then, the crucifixion never ends and we use Jesus to continue his death forever, killing others even, God forbid, in the name of Jesus.

Tolstoy, the Russian novelist, observed that the habits of the stone age are still strong in us. How fitting for Tolstoy to call the age of violence the stone age!

If we make Jesus a stone in our hands to hurl at the world, if we launch his message as a weapon against the other Christian churches, if we make Jesus the young David forever seeking a Goliath to slay, if Jesus becomes an excuse for violence against ourselves so that we ourselves have hearts of stone, then the crucifixion never ends and Easter has no place in our experience.

Tolstoy tells us that we may continue violence if we wish but we cannot do this in the name of Jesus.

The tomb of Jesus is sealed with stone. If the stones do not roll from our hands, then the tomb never opens.

Who will help us discard the stone of violence? Who will push it back for us so that Easter might happen and so that the world can be born again in water and the Spirit?

One of the most obvious signs of life is its vulnerability. Life is not hard as stone. On the other hand, the hardening of the human body into stone is a clear sign of death. The heart and the spirit die the same way. The only sin the Spirit cannot dislodge is a sin which makes the heart into stone and keeps the sin forever at its core, refusing to release it. The sin the Spirit cannot forgive is the sin of making the heart a weapon, a stone, to hurl forever at life.

Jesus is not expected to be a stone in our hands but the bread of life. When bread becomes hard as stone, it can no longer give life. For bread to nourish us, it must be broken; for a heart to love us, it must open itself. For a child to be born, there must be a way out of the womb; for Easter to happen, the tomb must be unsealed.

Violence will not do. Easter is the end of all violence; its promise is peace and pacifism.

As we use violence, the world becomes hard and the planet loses the resiliency of life. As the church becomes unyielding, people leave it and seek the bread of life elsewhere. They abandon the temple and find Christ on the road to Emmaus or in the evening shadows as bread is broken in gentleness and love.

The church is not to be a tomb of stone and order and silence but an upper room of bread and festivity and dialogue. The church is not to be the place where the body is bathed and prepared for burial but the room where the feet of the living are washed so that all can go forth on mission.

And, so, violence will not do.

If we speak of the unacceptability of violence, we need to consider the credibility of pacifism and nonviolence. Do they really work? Pacifism is often discredited as a viable option in our time because it lacks the realism and force of violence. People who speak of nonviolence are repeatedly judged irrelevant, quaint, or ethereal. Yet, nonviolence may be indispensable to the creation of contemporary spirituality.

There can be no effective nonviolence with others until we learn to be nonviolent with ourselves. Jesus did not intend that his mission and life should lead us to diminish and discount ourselves. He surely did not wish us to discard ourselves as one might a stone, to walk away from the lives we have made, to hide ourselves from our own experience and the sacred history of our own life story.

Thomas Merton once wrote that every birthday is a new theology. The church and the world must write its history and script its life differently as each person comes on the scene with unique gifts and personal needs.

We must go gently into our own lives and not ransack our own existence as if it were the enemy. There are no enemies. We must encounter forgiveness as something we are worthy to receive even as we are obliged to give it. We must accept all the moments, even the darkest, because they, too, have something to contribute. The reverses we suffer may fill us with compassion for all those whose lives are a crucifixion and may make our hope for Easter all the more ardent.

The most destructive violence we do in life is directed at ourselves. Terrified and timid, we sometimes live not the life we were given but the life someone else expects of us. In such cases, we lose our lives rather than affirm them. As we accuse ourselves and demean ourselves, we become hard as stone and make it impossible for our life to become bread for others. In spite of its fragility and flaws, a rose is one of the most beautiful forms of life on the planet. Ralph Waldo Emerson once observed that roses are a metaphor for our self-development. Each rose becomes, he noted, not what another rose tells it to become but what its own chemistry and destiny lead it to become. A rose does not look to another rose to create its beauty. It creates beauty from its own resources.

If we wish to give the world bread and roses, we must harvest first the bread and roses of our own lives. We must believe in the wheat and flowers of our existence. If we discard our lives, who will live them?

When we reject the goodness of our lives, when we are no longer capable of believing in ourselves and of being gentle with ourselves, then we make harsh institutions and severe laws and we seek to punish ourselves by serving them.

Nonviolence with ourselves means that we change and are always free. And so we are not easy to define. We are not categorized as just one thing, as this or that defect or this or that virtue. We are the sum total of all our experiences and of all that will continue to make us something different in the future.

Who taught us to be violent with ourselves? Certainly not Jesus. We were to love our neighbor as we already loved ourselves. We were to love one another as Jesus loved us. We were to walk away from condemnation and death, as the woman taken in adultery does.

Is it possible that this same woman became the anonymous woman who one day anointed the head of

Jesus with oil and washed his feet with her tears? Was Jesus inspired at the last supper to wash the feet of the disciples by the example of the anonymous woman?

In any case, we know she did not sit in the Sanhedrin. It is almost certain that some of those who did sit in the Sanhedrin and demanded the death of Jesus had shortly before demanded the death of the woman.

Nonviolence with ourselves is the first rubric in the liturgy of love, the keynote of a life song. Nonviolence with ourselves makes possible and inevitable nonviolence with others.

The sacred triduum of Holy Thursday, Good Friday, Easter Vigil is the school in which we are to learn nonviolence. In this experience, Jesus becomes bread for life; he becomes a word of forgiveness from the cross; and he brings Easter glory and peace without violence, belligerence or even struggle.

We must not be tempted to suppose that violence makes the world better or safer or that it ultimately solves all problems. Indeed, we might argue that violence always loses, in the human scale of values, because it always requires a victim. For the victim and the victim's network of relationships, violence is often a devastating loss, one which does not justify the so-called good results which derive from it. A system or solution which starts with violence tends to search out victims when it is threatened again. It counts its victories, all too frequently, in terms of how many people have lost their lives, of how much damage is done, of how thoroughly the enemy is humiliated and controlled. It sets up a cycle of vengeance and retaliation which is self-perpetuating and even everlasting until someone breaks the cycle with peace and forgiveness.

There are other liabilities and weaknesses to violence. Violence transforms the self into a cruel person and deprives the world of what that person might have become otherwise. The ecology of the human heart, so to speak, is degraded until love itself becomes an endangered species. Compassion and mercy are aborted as the misbegotten children of whatever new world order is conceived.

Violence defeats itself sooner or later, creating enemies by its own devices. These enemies learn the lessons of destruction and killing, schooled by an environment of savagery which counsels victory at all costs and makes winning everything.

Ten million people were killed in World War I, another fifty million in World War II, and more than twenty-five million in conficts which followed. This total of eighty-five million people, a number beyond the ability of the human mind to comprehend in any concrete manner, is only a partial list of those destroyed; others perished by violence in everyday life. These people died one by one, as human beings, not as statistics or cumulative numbers. They died as children and mothers, as friends and husbands. Networks of relationships and whole families were shattered by their violent deaths.

Yet we continue to believe that violence works. We persist in this conviction because violence seduces us with its efficiency and its ability to eliminate those we do not wish to exist in our world. It entices us with the illusion that we are God and that it is ours to decide who should live and who should not. It tempts us with the supposed equity and contrived fairness of an eye for an eye, a victim for a victim, a life for a life.

Gandhi once observed that when we demand an eye for an eye we soon make the whole world blind.

Eventually, all this violence against others leads us to question our own worth. It makes us insecure as enemies are multiplied. It creates, subtly but surely, a deep hatred of ourselves.

The Christian community in the beginning was nonviolent. It observed pacifism for centuries. This emphasis on peace was inspired by the events which transpired in the Paschal season.

Jesus took the sword out of Peter's hand and turned his cheek so that Judas might kiss him in betrayal. Jesus washed the feet of those about to desert him and forgave those who nailed his own feet to the cross. Jesus appeared on Easter morning with no stones of accusation but with the bread of peace and the roses of reconciliation. His wounds were not used as weapons to wound others.

Christianity expected no one to serve in the Roman army. There is no record of resistance by Christians to those who persecuted them. With the word of God in their hearts and bread in their hands, with communities of love and celebrations inviting all to the table, early, nonviolent Christianity prevailed in Jerusalem, Athens and Rome. No one would have imagined as Jesus was put to death by Roman soldiers that one day the emperor would ask for baptism in the name of Jesus.

What enemy, we might ask, sowed Christianity's fertile fields of peace with seeds of destruction and violence? Who introduced weeds into the wheat so that Christianity could no longer tell the difference between violence and the following of Christ? How did Christianity come to disregard the lilies of the field, the gentle breaking of bread, the forgiveness of enemies and the washing of feet, for weapons and stones, for engines of death and implements of rage? What heresy entered our devotional system and poisoned the waters of life which sprang up from Jesus? Why

44

did we justify war rather than the beatitudes and pro-claim crusades rather than forgiveness seventy times seven?

The changes may have been due primarily to two factors, both of them emerging in the fourth century.

The first of these tragic events was the fascination with power and the addiction to legality which came with Constantine. In a sense, Constantine tempted the Christian community with the last temptation of Christ in the desert. "The devil showed him all the kingdoms of the world and said: 'I will give you all this' . . ." The Christian church accepted what Jesus refused in the wilderness. With power came the sword. The hun-ger now was less for bread than for stones, less for the word of God than for weapons.

It is not coincidental that a few generations after Constantine, Augustine elaborates the theology of just wars. It is possible, Augustine argued, to take up the sword, to fight in the Roman army, to kill with virtue and do God's will by violence. This may be virtuous as long as we do not intend the killing we are doing. We must kill for the values the killing will assure.

Thomas Merton observes that Augustine's just-war theory depends upon a spiritual schizophrenia which divorces our act of killing from the consequences suf-fered by the victim. Killing is made into the collateral damage of instilling virtue. The killing is somehow sought and unintended simultaneously.

This thinking disregards the wounds of the victim and concentrates on some ideal the killer seeks. It is as heretical as early Docetism, which claimed Jesus never had a body so that his death and wounds were illusions, able to be ignored, items of little consequence.

Just-war theories led the church to justify inquisitions and crusades, ghettoes and torture, wars and executions. These theories permitted Christians to kill in the name of God and for the sake of peace. They made the core of Christ's message somehow irrelevant. Killing became the price we paid, like thirty pieces of silver, for having Christ where we needed him to be.

With power and just-war theories, we are tempted to rely on law as more trustworthy than charism and community. The Roman emperors were enamored of law and justified their killing by it. They judged themselves compassionate if they followed procedures and rules, if they allowed trials and evidence before they executed the condemned. Law retains the capacity to convince people they have acted ethically, even generously, if they abide by its statutes. The law unquestionably, properly utilized, brings a measure of humaneness and tranquillity into our relationships with one another. It easily blinds us to people, however, and limits our involvement with them to structured categories, at best; it allows us, at worst, to become cruel with one another. It was this dimension of the law the gospel resisted. It is ironic, even tragic, that the Christian community has made so much of the law and done this in the name of the very Jesus who insisted often on a larger perspective. Law easily becomes the first choice of those who have given up on community.

There is a second element responsible for our abandonment of nonviolence as a credible way to live. This was also a fourth-century development in its origins, and likewise found Augustine an eager propagandist. We are speaking now of the devaluation of women.

Augustine's problems with sexual discipline, his

obsessive eroticism and promiscuity, his seventeen-year cohabitation with a mistress who became the mother of his son, these experiences led Augustine to view women and sexuality as threats and temptations. He came to propose celibacy as the ideal way for a Christian to live.

The woman whom Augustine lived with was executed in his heart as he sought to rid himself of her and of all women. He never names her. She is as anonymous as the woman taken in adultery. Augustine feared lust, almost pathologically, and became angry at his vulnerability before it. He blamed women and marriage as well as himself. He counselled married men to avoid sex with their wives or, if they must have sex, to express themselves without passion or intensity.

Augustine's teaching amounted to a violation of women. Sex without love or passion or even much interest is rape by another name. Augustine was violent with himself and this led him to violence with others. Marriage became a battlefield for just-war tactics. One might have sex as long as one did not intend pleasure or regard the partner. The ideal pursued became more important than the damage to the victim.

The collateral damage of sex is original sin. Original sin is transmitted by sexual intercourse, Augustine argues. If there were no sex, the world would be free of evil. Original sin was a kind of AIDS virus infecting the children of Christian parents who were too weak for a celibate marriage and too lustful to refrain from sex. Augustine does not link marital sex with love or grace or the gospel.

Marriage is for pitiable Christians, ruled by genital needs and dishonorable drives. The infection of original sin would be less, Augustine reasoned, if Christians made love disinterestedly. The less the passion in conception the less the infection of sin in the child. Yet every child, no matter how indifferent the parents in conceiving it, came into the world as evil, destined for hell, the object of God's unrelenting anger. Only baptism could rescue a child from this disease and from eternal punishment. Augustine insisted against a group of heretics, as he viewed them, called Pelagians that every unbaptized child burned forever in hell. He told the Pelagians, to their astonishment, that God was repelled by the sight and the nearness of the unbaptized. The newborn infant, fresh from the sex and passion of its parents, was, in reality, a moral monstrosity.

Augustine, of course, had better moments. The Christian community which endorsed these doctrines must also be indicted. In any case power and just-war theories, the devaluation of women and the primacy of law, the denigration of sexual experience and the justification of violence as virtue enter the bloodstream of the Christian community.

Nonviolence may be the best remedy against power and harsh laws, against the degradation of women and human sexuality and marriage.

Nonviolence is sometimes less appealing because it does not achieve its results on our schedule. It is less in our control and fits less neatly into our planning.

Nonviolence follows a different agenda and accounting. It achieves its objective in a season and a manner less predictable. The captivity of the woman taken in adultery is easier to control than her freedom. To recall our analogy, violence is as measurable as the size and shape of a stone; nonviolence has about it the ambiguity and unpredictability of forgiveness.

Nonviolence generates an impressive capacity for creativity and resiliency. Violence is often done the same way with everyone and anyone. Nonviolence requires calibration and fine-tuning, imagination and sensitivity to the other and to the changing conditions of life.

Nonviolence reaches us on levels deeper than the law (which it often resists), on levels more profound than reason. It cannot explain itself in logical categories as readily as violence can.

Nonviolence requires us to regard the other not as an enemy but as someone we must liberate before we ourselves can be free. Unless the other is forgiven, we shall never absolve ourselves. Nonviolence does not divide the human family into adversaries and allies but considers everyone a partner.

Saturday vigil. The cross is deserted; Christ is contained and controlled in the tomb. Violence has done its worst. Jesus, however, has taken the mystique and allure of violence out of it by his dying and forgiveness. He offers, instead, love as a norm and trust in life even when the odds against it are overwhelming. Reason assures us that Jesus is finished and that violence has prevailed. Saturday vigil is for those prepared to wait for a better interpretation of life and a new revelation of its power. Saturday is for those who seek a future beyond the limits of law and power. It is a sabbath of the Spirit for a community of invincible hope.

MEDITATIONS

5

Good Friday:
Personalities Under Pressure

They were young men of sharp contrasts and surprising similarities. Both grew up in Galilee and so they had a lot in common. They were idealists; most who followed Jesus were. They were with him from the beginning; there was some prestige attached to such things. There was no way to know how badly it would end. Idealists seldom consider negative possibilities.

Galilee was hardly the cultural capital of the world. Its citizens discussed fishing and farming more readily than they did law, politics and theology.

Judas and Peter must have talked often about the weather and harvests, about the run of fish in the lake and the simple days when life was less complex. They were moved by Jesus and defined by him; yet they kept enough distance to assert themselves when their own interests or fears suddenly emerged. They had a lot in common. People could notice the unspoken connections between them. Perhaps Peter felt temperamentally closer to Andrew or John, but Judas and Peter were leaders and strong personalities. Both could criticize actions of Jesus and did so. One seemed to be a person other men and women trusted readily; the other was astute enough to calculate and manage the financial affairs of the small group. Both had a sense of the extremism of Jesus at times: Peter cautioned him against his readiness to die or even to wash their feet; Judas saw Jesus as politically naive and fiscally improvident.

For three years, Peter and Judas ate, discussed and debated together. They helped change each other's perceptions and judgments. They slept in the open fields, heard the parables, wondered and worried about the strong effect Jesus had on the crowds.

In spite of all this, something went very wrong between them. We remember them differently. They are so opposite in our recollection of them that it is not easy to realize how close they had been, especially during those times when the whole world, it seemed, was against them. In the final hours of the life of Jesus, Judas and Peter played roles that were strikingly similar. Under pressure, they were more alike than the others in the circle of the Twelve.

Both men betrayed their basic loyalty to Jesus when he needed them most. Both knew how unreliable they could become when courage and fidelity were demanded of them. Both suffered severely from a sense of their own unworthiness.

Both chose violence in the garden the night of the arrest. Judas led a band with lanterns, torches and weapons. Peter carried a sword, in spite of all Jesus had said; he knew how to use it; he cut off a man's ear, the gospels remind us. Not a very nice memory. Peter was armed and threatening when need be. The victim was no less than the servant of the high priest; such an action would not dispose the high priest to a favorable judgment in hearing the case of Jesus. The betrayal began for Peter in the garden, with mutilation, bloodshed and desertion. Peter must have wondered if he had learned anything at all from Jesus, as he reflected on all this in silence and trembling. Jesus may have asked himself the same questions about Peter.

The crucifixion of Jesus was a defining event for both men. Surely, Judas never anticipated such horror. He may have been fractured with moral fault lines through his psyche; capable of stealing and deception, of greed and manipulation. He was not, however, a cold person who could walk away apathetically from the devastation he had caused. Such men do not commit suicide.

Peter must have come close to despair as he heard of the awful execution of Jesus. He was a leader who became a coward at the time of testing. He led his men into desertion. He lied time and again throughout the ordeal. It is not too much to wonder whether he, too, considered suicide. How would he be able to live the rest of his life with the nightmares of Jesus nailed to the cross and his own behavior etched indelibly into his memory?

With so much in common, we would not have conjectured, had we known them in life, that Judas and Peter would have been evaluated as almost complete opposites of each other. Why, we might ask, do we honor one, and distance ourselves from the other? If someone compares us to Judas, we are offended; if we are linked with Peter, we are complimented.

Why the difference?

Judas at some point, for reasons we cannot discern, stopped believing in love and forgiveness. He may have judged himself unworthy of both; the enormity of the betrayal may have overwhelmed his capacity to see anyone or anything else. He may have sought to kill his sin and the memory of it as he did away with himself.

Peter betrayed love also but did not allow his belief in love to die. The ultimate tragedy of Judas was not the act of evil but the lack of faith. Peter's strength was not his courage but his conviction that Jesus would always find a place for him.

It is never beyond the realm of possibility that we might betray Christ or those we love as callously as Judas did. In one instance, we must be most careful not to imitate Judas. We must always believe we are forgivable; we must never despair of love.

The church repeats the tragedy of Judas not only when it betrays the gospel but worse, when it sends away the people who look for Christ in the church. In failing to find room in the inn for everyone, the church dismisses not only the stranger who comes to it for help, but Christ himself whom it no longer recognizes. Some believers come among their own and their own receive them not.

The church must find a place of honor and respect for those who turn to it. To give a believer the crumbs from the table, reserved for the dogs, is hardly to imitate Christ. Dorothy Day once observed that the charity the state is obliged by law to dispense often demeans the people it should be assisting. This is not acceptable in the church. Unless the church gives people a sense they are members of the family, it dismembers the Body of Christ. There is a world of difference between those who "love" us for their own sake and those who love us as we need to be loved. The church may not always be capable of loving as it should, but it must always sense the difference between its institutional priorities and the personal requirements of others.

Unless Peter can weep for Judas as well as for himself, he has not yet become the Faithful Shepherd.

BARABBAS AND JOSEPH OF ARIMATHEA

One is a murderer. He gains from the death of Jesus. If Jesus is executed, he is a free man. So be it. Life is harsh and cruel. He wants Jesus dead so he can get out of prison. He neither knows nor cares about Jesus. Jesus is a means to an end, a way of getting to what he wants. Barabbas is a recognizable type. In some ways, he is all of us.

Joseph of Arimathea is a respected person, a member of the Sanhedrin, as prestigious a position as any reasonable person could hope to achieve. In modern terms, being in the Sanhedrin was similar to belonging to the United States Senate, the Supreme Court and the College of Cardinals all at once. The Sanhedrin was the supreme legislative, judicial and religious assembly in Jerusalem. There was a lot to protect, a great deal one must be careful not to lose.

For Joseph, the death of Jesus will not create personal advantages.

The trial of Jesus involves him in a sharp controversy (not good for a politician). It identifies him with a criminal, indeed one who is executed after three trials (before the Sanhedrin, Herod Antipas and Pilate) and an interrogation at the home of the former chief priest, Annas.

Nonetheless, Joseph of Arimathea comes forward and offers his own tomb for the burial of Jesus. The gratitude of the early disciples is obvious; he is mentioned in the gospel tradition and cited by name when the narratives of Jesus' life are written.

Today, we honor Joseph of Arimathea and we distance ourselves from Barabbas. Both of them, nonetheless, leave us with questions.

Would we ourselves accept release if we were guilty of murder and aware that an innocent man would die in our place? If we did allow such to occur, would we be proud of this turn of events, able to look our children in the eye? Would we feel good about ourselves as we reflected on all this? Could we make it through life without nightmares, tension headaches, shame?

There is such a difference between asking ourselves what we can get out of someone else's misfortune and what we might do to help someone who has suffered! Barabbas goes free and Jesus dies. Life brings advantages, often at someone else's expense.

Joseph reasons differently. There is not much to offer. A tomb. It shows he cares. People may not be happy with him for what he does. The horror of the execution, the injustice of it, the grief on the mother's face, the helplessness and hopelessness of it all! A tomb is not much but it does make a difference. The death cannot be stopped but the brutality of it can be lessened. Every time someone offers mercy the world is better for all of us.

PILATE AND CAIAPHAS

They should have been very different; Pilate, a Roman official, a man publicly dedicated to power and politics; Caiaphas, a Jew and a priest, representing a God of mercy and justice.

They grew up in antagonistic worlds, nurtured in cultures which looked condescendingly at each other, trained in systems which convinced them their tradition was the standard for all people.

They should have been very different. They were not. Sometimes, religion and politics are the same reality, with different words, and God becomes an excuse for what one does or does not do for one's personal advantage.

Pilate and Caiaphas were the major leaders of their own institutions in the capital city of Jerusalem. One always knew what the other was doing, though they pretended not to care. In power games, one pays more attention to one's enemies and adversaries than to one's friends. Things were not very different, then or now.

Both men gave their lives to having a decisive influence over others, whatever the mixed motives may have been which led them to this choice. They were successful. How did they handle their impressive career achievements?

We see them in the gospel account at a critical juncture in their lives. They send an innocent man to his death. Since the gospel record is the only one we have, we shall stay with that, seeking to avoid its sometimes partisan interpretation of those who order the execution.

Caiaphas might argue that he was protecting the temple and the Jewish religion by eliminating a critic of both. Yet, we might observe, systems which are sound are no more threatened by dissenters than a healthy organism is with the diseases which assail it. Jesus is never charged with armed resistance or lethal force against the institution. One is left with the impression that what was being threatened was not so much a sacred reality but the status and power base of a man, Caiaphas, who wanted to be in control. Words are not able to be threatening unless they are somehow true and unless people at large already want things to be different. Sound institutions, like healthy people and good marriages, grow from criticism.

Pilate might insist that he was preserving law and order. Yet, clearly, a preacher from Galilee whose basic message was directed at internal renewal of the human spirit was no threat to Rome. The problem for Pilate was not Jesus but the power players who would make trouble for Pilate if Jesus were not executed. The prisoner may have been interrogated by Pilate but the focus of attention was a constituency Pilate feared he could not control.

Both Caiaphas and Pilate choose a victim rather than considering the weakness in their own systems and in their own lives. The temple and the Jewish system of priesthood and sacrifice, which Caiaphas championed, will come to a decisive end, never to be restored, within some forty years of the crucifixion. Pilate will be summoned to Rome and forced to commit suicide before the emperor some eight years after sending Jesus to his death.

In the clash between the system and the truth, Caiaphas and Pilate chose the system. In the conflict between barbarism and mercy, they chose barbarism. Even the ruthless Romans saw crucifixion as the most horrible form of death imaginable.

Caiaphas and Pilate were very much alike.

They thought they were different. For Pilate, the emperor was everything. He had the emperor's favor. The Roman province of Palestine was not unimportant. Later, two men, Vespasian and Titus, will become emperors because of their work in Palestine. Pilate is on a fast track. It is important that no one make him look ineffective. Rome does not care about the death of a Galilean, but it will be disturbed if Pilate seems unable to keep his province in check.

For Caiaphas, God, the Torah and the prophets were supposedly his central commitment. He had done well with his calling. Indeed, being chief priest was becoming a family tradition. He had married the daughter of the previous chief priest and his father-in-law remained a powerful even if less visible presence. If someone on the margins of Jewish life, a carpenter from Galilee, were crucified, few in the establishment would take notice. Indeed, the chief priest would seem to be doing his job; his zealotry for the Torah and the temple, his indignation against blasphemy, would play well in the marketplace. The death of Jesus would be as insignificant as the stoning of an anonymous adulteress. The law is the law; and the chief priest is the guardian.

Caiaphas and Pilate had a lot to protect. They would understand each other even if their public roles kept them at a distance. They should have been as different as two men could be. They were not.

Questions could be asked of us. Are we much different from those who do not believe in God or accept Christ? Has the law of love made our lives exemplary? Is the church more compassionate than the state, more honest, more trustworthy? Are these questions legitimate questions? What answers do we make and why do we answer as we do? Is there more of Caiaphas and Pilate in us and in the church than we would like?

THE SOLDIERS AND NICODEMUS

One way to look at this cast of characters is through economics.

The soldiers are given extra pay for carrying out executions, especially crucifixions. A lot of soldiers wanted to have nothing to do with such savage work.

It was messy business, nailing a man to a cross. One came away sometimes with blood and vomit and spit all over one's uniform. The shrieking of the condemned and his family or friends was not pleasant. Breaking a man's legs with clubs was brutal.

Then, there was the tedium. Waiting around a cross for three days was boring. Playing dice passed the time but how long could one do that?

There were other inducements to coax soldiers to do this job. One got to keep the clothes of the criminal, sometimes a piece of jewelry perhaps. On other occasions, relatives would bribe the soldiers to make things easier for the dying man. Since relatives were not in a strong negotiating position, the soldiers could do well. For the most part, however, people sent to crucifixion were the dregs of society, seldom wealthy, often without family or friends who cared about them.

The soldiers who crucified Jesus did not get much. His garments were divided four ways. There was no jewelry. Hardly any family or friends kept vigil. There was no money to spare for bribes.

The pay, nonetheless, was good. Someone always seems to gain from someone else's losses.

When Jesus dies, an unexpected patron arrives. Nicodemus is a wealthy man and, remarkably, a member of the Sanhedrin.

Nicodemus brings with him one hundred pounds of myrrh, aloes, spices, oils, perfumes for the burial. John's gospel describes the entombment as the burial of a king. Nicodemus, in this account, is lavish, extravagant, generous, almost reckless. Not knowing how accurate the portrayal is, we work with the story, nonetheless.

Nicodemus is a contrast to the soldiers. He does not take from the tragedy but gives. He does not seek a personal advantage from the horror but looks for a way to help. He does not make money but disposes of it.

Indeed, he donates more than money. He puts himself on the line.

Questions for ourselves arise again. Do we take or give with those we love? If we are generous, is it only with money or also with ourselves, our time, our attention, our respect and compassion?

What did Nicodemus see in Jesus to have risked so much for him? Had we been Nicodemus, with the same assets and the same status, what would we have done? Might we not have judged that Jesus lost the trial and now his life and, therefore, any jeopardy to ourselves on his behalf would not be worth the cost? Perhaps a letter to the mother of the crucified, or a kind word to a friend or disciple of Jesus would be sufficient. No one else would have to know about that. There are people and causes in life which we need to support from a distance, even though we believe in them, if we wish to make our way to the top of whatever institutions we espouse.

THE WOMEN

Three of them are named. All of them are called "Mary." One, the mother of Jesus, had lost a husband and, now, a son. She has a sister, Mary, who is with her at the cross. Mary Magdalene completes the circle.

They watch. Helpless. Yet they exhibit astonishing courage. The weakest become the strongest. Society had defined women as dependent, vulnerable. They are at the cross on their own, independent, self-contained, faithful to the end. They do not carry a sword, as Peter did; and he is absent. Nor did they betray their friend, as Judas did. They do not gain an advantage from the death of Jesus, as Barabbas did or as the soldiers do. They do not use the death of Jesus to assist their careers, as Caiaphas and Pilate do. They do not run away. Nor do they call attention to themselves. They are there because they are needed and because they are devoted to Christ.

If we seek an icon of strength and endurance, we find a better expression of it in these women and their nonviolence than we do in Peter with a weapon or Judas with his silver or Caiaphas with his priestly robes or Pilate with his Roman insignia or the soldiers with their hammers and nails. The apparently strong are weak and do not prevail. Who wishes to remember them as they were then or present them as models to imitate?

Questions again remain. They must be allowed to surface and to be held in the mind and heart even when they cannot be answered.

Had we sat in the Sanhedrin and judged a carpenter from Nazareth who broke the law and lost his following, would we have risked everything to set him free, even if we suspected his innocence? Would we find convenient excuses, facile rationalizations? If the chief priest and a large majority favored a sentence of death, would we be strong enough, willing enough to resist?

Would we have voted for death or acquittal? Think of it.

Where would we have been as the execution began? Think of it.

6

An Easter Homily

Let us begin by gathering the fragments.
Life is an experience of bits and pieces. Too often we want it to be complete before its time.

A child in the womb is put together in bits and pieces. It is not entire all at once. Even when the child is born, it is not finished.

To want life to be whole without delay, on our timetable and with our priorities, is an act of violence. It violates the integrity of others and assaults them with our agenda. Nonviolence allows life to follow its due tempo, to mark its seasons, to be partial in its answers and unfulfilled in some of its promises. The violent rush life through its paces, impose rigid ideologies upon it, present it with impossible ideals, and reduce it to a frenzy of impatience and disillusionment. The nonviolent know how to wait and they trust the process and the timing. The nonviolent become contemplative with life and learn reverence from it. The violent are judgmental about life, always quantifying it, deciding whether it measures up or not, cataloguing its successes and failures. The nonviolent are attentive to life and responsive, sensitive to its rhythms and aware that what we consider failures are often successes in another form.

No one of us gets life all at once and no one of us should.

Life is a gathering of fragments, a crazy quilt tapestry of bits and pieces which fit even when we think they should not and which, of course, is never finished. There is always another possibility.

To have life whole is to allow it no further opportunities. The violent want life to be controlled, finished, predictable. They trap life and people. The nonviolent create alternatives. They allow us to have life in fragments and, therefore, always make a different future possible.

In the three days of Holy Week, we deal with the bits and pieces of life, the fragments of Christ's meaning for us. We learn, if we are receptive, that we must be satisfied with partial answers and incomplete explanations. We come to live with half-guesses and unresolved melodies. At moments, we have a sense of the truth of the whole, but it is not something we can explain or even achieve.

We are given some of the pieces on Thursday in the lamb and the wine, the broken bread and the empty cup, the washing of feet, the vine and the branches, the night in the garden, the arrest in the moonlight.

A Christ of fragments begins to emerge but it is all very tentative and hesitant.

On Friday, the most disconcerting fragment of all, the one which seems to fit with none of the other pieces, the torn body and bruised heart, the withered spirit and cries for companionship from the cross, the darkened sun and the desertion of the disciples, the desperate closeness of death. Mary holds him for the last time and Magdalene watches where they bury him.

A Christ of fragments. This is the only Christ we are given and allowed to receive.

Most of us want another Christ, a whole Christ, a Christ who provides all the answers, a Christ of total victory and no enemies, a Christ of light so luminous that it banishes all shadows, a Christ of the Second Coming even before the First is complete.

Here at the tomb, on a Saturday before Easter, an Advent sabbath, we wait in confusion. This Christmas passover has no room for Christ, it seems. Once denied an inn for his birth, now he is refused the right to live anywhere in our world.

It is urgent for Christ and for us and for the church that we not expect too much too soon, that we allow Jesus to be Jesus and our own life to evolve without forcing the timing, the tempo and the meaning.

Our church calls itself the Body of Christ, realized in us, his members. We must not expect the church at large, the people of God, to be whole, to have all the answers, to be darkened by no shadows, to come up with all the pieces and fit them together correctly. Our church is a church of fragments if it is Christ's church as well.

This is all as it should be for us. No one of our lives is a whole event, an entire life. All of our lives are in the making, bits and pieces arranged in patterns which we seldom anticipate and sometimes do not even elect. Each of us is being assembled once again as we once were in the womb, in bits and pieces we neither foresee nor choose.

In the jigsaw puzzle of our personal lives, there are lights and shadows, sin and grace, days of docility and seasons of dissent, psychological landscapes of devotion and aridity, hopes which give life and memories which seem to take it away.

The worst mistake we make is in holding on to only one part as though it were everything. It is wrong to stop the process before it is finished. That would be like terminating a pregnancy before its time.

There is a Buddhist parable about a young widower who lost his young son to bandits. They came to his house when he was away and burned it to the ground. Among the ashes, he found the charred remains of a child and kept the ashes in a velvet bag near his heart. Working, sleeping, eating, he carried the ashes with him. They were his son.

One day, his real son escaped the bandits and found his way home. He arrived at his father's house at midnight and knocked joyously at the door. "Papa, I'm home. I'm your son. Let me in."

The father thought someone was playing a cruel joke. He began to cry because of his pain and told the tormentor to go away. He clutched the bag of ashes.

The son continued to knock and the father refused to admit him. Time passed.

Finally the son left.

The father, certain he knew the form and shape of his son, would find his son only in the ashes.

The father and son never met again.

Sometimes we take a part of the truth to be the whole truth. We do not let other possibilities in, new pieces of the puzzle, other fragments of life, different moments and configurations, surprising patterns.

If we cling to only one part, we lose the totality which is forming.

The Easter Vigil offers us choices. Some may choose to believe that Christ is wholly in the tomb and that the dead Christ is the only Christ there is. These are often the same people who conclude that their lives essentially come to an end at certain specified points, even if they are still living, and that nothing new can or ought to happen. Such people expect no more surprises and anticipate a future which is predictable. For them, hope is foolish. Christ is entombed forever in the closed world they inhabit and the narrow lives they prefer. They also want a church which never changes, a church always the same.

But the Christ of the Fragments assures us that the shards and syllables have meanings, not as isolated units but together. The face of Christ keeps changing as the Body of Christ takes on different members and new meanings. The whole church is pregnant with Christ throughout its entire history.

As the three women come to the tomb on Easter morning, they find it empty. The death of Christ, they learn, was only a fragment. "He is ahead of you already," the angel declares in the gospel.

Death is but one of the fragments of life. All the pieces are important. We must not lose any of them or settle for only one of them.

The syllables of our lives will one day come together as a whole scripture. This is the hope Easter engenders. The bread of our existence will one day be unbroken; the mosaic of our experience will fit together as a chalice to hold the new wine of Christ.

Easter assures us that the tapestry of our lives is woven from all its parts and that none of the threads is useless. Everything fits and has a meaning.

The tomb is empty now.

Jesus is elsewhere as the Christ who is more patient with the pieces of his life and ours than we are.

When all the parts are assembled, Christ will see in us his own face and the members of his body.

He will open the door where we had knocked in

panic. He will know us as his sons and daughters who are still living and, therefore, need not be sought in the ashes of death. As the door opens, we shall find that we know the place for the first time as the home we longed to live in for as long as we can remember.

7

Sunrise

It was dark as Mary Magdalene made her way through the streets of Jerusalem and then headed outside the city. This was to be her first return to the tomb, near Calvary, since the horror of Friday afternoon. It was dark then also as she left the place of execution.

John's gospel is the only one which notes the presence of Mary, the mother of Jesus, at the cross. She is there, we are told, with her sister and with Magdalene.

Magdalene must have looked a number of times at Mary of Nazareth during the dying of Jesus. John's gospel, alone, records words of Jesus from the cross to his mother: "Woman, look at your son." Surely, Magdalene gazed in the direction of Mary during that tender and tragic moment.

In the midst of the shock and violence of Friday, the quiet, silent presence of the women is a nonviolent interlude, an oasis of tranquillity in a landscape of waste and desolation. They form the contemplative center of a world gone mad, it seems, with frenzy and bloodshed. They say and do nothing. Yet, they become, simply by their being there, a sanctuary of pacifism in the tumult and terror around them.

Women are especially effective with nonviolence. The first recorded act of nonviolent resistance is found in the Bible, in the opening chapter of Exodus. Hebrew midwives refuse to implement Pharaoh's orders to kill male children born to Hebrew mothers. When they are summoned to Pharaoh to explain why infant boys are alive and growing, they tell him that Hebrew women are hardier than Egyptians and deliver their children before the midwives arrive.

Pharaoh is frustrated by the passive resistance and rendered powerless by their unstated noncompliance. One of the Hebrew boys rescued through this nonviolence is Moses.

As Magdalene walks the dark and quiet streets, she seeks the tomb of Jesus whom the gospel will later present as a new Moses for a new covenant community.

Moses was fortunate by comparison. No one tore off his clothes and nailed him to a tree. The mother of Moses did not have to watch her son die a tortured and savage death.

Moses died in honor, buried in the land of Moab, one hundred and twenty years old, we are told, "his eye undimmed, his vigor unimpaired."

The new Moses, the young carpenter from Nazareth, dies in the vigor of his youth, a criminal, rejected, brokenhearted. One could not imagine new life or a future community from such a turn of events!

Magdalene is near the tomb now.

Why could Jesus not have lived as long as Moses? Why is there no one to mourn this young prophet?

Magdalene looks up and is astonished. The stone has moved!

She does not enter the tomb but runs panic-stricken through the streets of Jerusalem. "Peter, I must find Peter," she cries in her heart. "Peter," she gasps as she finds him, "he's gone; the body, it's gone;

someone took him from the tomb. We don't know where they put him."

The "we" is the first indication that someone else had been with Magdalene. Could it have been Mary of Nazareth?

Peter runs to the tomb and enters it.

She must have returned with Peter.

On this second visit, while she is distraught, confused, weeping, a young man expresses concern for her. "O, Sir, where have they put the body? Why did they do this? Do you know where he is? Can anyone tell me?"

"Mary," he replies. She looks up, startled, and cries out in joy, "Rabboni!"

She knows the shepherd's voice and the shepherd knows the sheep by name.

Then, he is gone.

Magdalene finds an empty tomb on her first visit. She now has a full heart.

"Jesus is risen," she tells the disciples. "I have seen him; we have spoken; he is here again."

Magdalene is the first to proclaim the resurrection. Perhaps this is why she is mentioned more than any other woman in the gospel narratives.

This tender encounter of Magdalene and Jesus takes away from us the anger and vengeance we might have felt for what was done to Jesus. Her faith and devotion bring us peace.

Moses died in honor. But Jesus, the new Moses, dies only for a time.

He is risen now. All the world knows this.

As he appears to his disciples, he says not a word about the violence done to him. He indicts none of the disciples for their desertion and cowardice.

He greets them in peace.

There is light in the sky now. It is Easter morning. The sun conquers the night, without a weapon. The sun need only be present for the darkness to recoil.

The Easter Christ is not really active. There are no miracles. It is the presence of the Son, without a weapon, indeed with wounds not yet healed, which makes the difference.

Love conquers by its nearness, by its presence.

In the light, on the horizon of the planet in the inner recesses of our hearts, Christ is present once more. The violence, the weapons, the angry words, the evil thoughts recoil.

Peace has proved itself invincible.

O Rabboni!!!

EPILOGUE

It has twice been my privilege to conduct a Holy Week retreat for the Sisters of Charity of Convent Station, New Jersey at St. Elizabeth's College. The 1986 retreat became a book, Christmas to Calvary *(Paulist Press), comparing the themes of convergence in the gospels between the birth stories and the death narratives. We tried to show how the accounts of the beginning of the life of Jesus and its end were symbolically and substantively linked.*

The 1991 retreat, organized around the theme of Scripture in the Streets, *raises questions about contemporary spirituality and nonviolence, about the role of women and the place of social justice.*

In addition to conferences and homilies, the retreat included liturgical ceremonies and two films. On Holy Thursday evening, Babette's Feast *was shown; an hour lecture and discussion developed the Holy Thursday theme of this apparently secular but deeply religious film about dining as celebration and transformation. On Good Friday evening,* The Mission, *based on historical fact, was presented; the ensuing session analyzed the film's message of nonviolence, sacrifice and redemption.*

One of the most compelling features of this retreat was a daily ritual conducted with stones.

The first conference, on Wednesday evening, deals with an imminent execution by stoning, of a woman taken in adultery. Each participant was invited to come forward at the end and drop a heavy stone into an iron bucket as a sign that violence and judgmental attitudes were rejected. The sound of the stones resounding through the silent chapel was a homily in its own right.

On Thursday, the theme was "Bread and Roses." Small loaves of bread were baked and, at the conclusion of the conference, each participant was asked to trade a stone for bread as the anthem "Bread and Roses" was sung. Jesus once noted that we do not give those we love a stone when bread is needed. Bread, of course, is a special Holy Thursday symbol.

On Friday, participants were asked to reassemble a pile of rocks into a cross as they came forward one by one. The cross was the sign of death which occurs when weapons are preferred to bread and when stones are not discarded.

On Saturday, the cross of stones became a new structure as a mound was formed. People were asked to meditate on whether the mound was a grave in which Jesus was forever dead, or whether the mound was a mountain of resurrection and new life.

At the Easter sunrise eucharist, the bucket, the stones, the bread and roses and wine became reminders of the entire retreat experience.

Scripture seems to evoke rituals. This scripture is most effective when it is proclaimed, conventionally, in the churches and also, innovatively, in the streets. Rituals also are best when they are a blend of the traditional and the new, the familiar and the startling.